Updated 2018

> *"Leadership is a choice, not a label."*
> **Bob 'Idea Man' Hooey**

Getting started

Welcome fellow leaders! Welcome to the *never-ending* journey of an evolving career and management focus on ***personal leadership development*** and coaching. A striking change in global perspective has placed a new focus and pressure on finding and applying more productive uses of your assets and updating your team members' skills to compete successfully.

Taking personal leadership in your own career growth and success is worth the investment. This is where you apply *leverage* to dynamically succeed! Too many leaders are *blind* to the opportunities and responsibilities of creating and nurturing those who would follow them. Too many miss the opportunity (*are blind*) to play an active part in the selection, growth, and success of those who would succeed them; those who would help them succeed as leaders.

> *"Avoid being the blind leading the blind ...*
> *leave behind a 'Legacy of Leadership'."*
> **Bob 'Idea Man' Hooey**

Leadership can be a *lonely* and *frustrating* road to walk. There will be times when you wonder if it is *worth the effort*. I know I have! **'LEAD! – 12 idea-rich leadership success strategies'** is my small contribution to helping you work through the frustrations, challenges, and lessons; to see your efforts bear positive fruit.

Being a persuasive and effective leader is a lifetime commitment and we need you.

LEAD! was written to share a few ideas, tips, and techniques we felt would be helpful in your quest for leadership significance.

In recent history, workplace coaching has taken on a new, more effective focus. Leading edge employees, managers, and successful executives have experienced positive results from enlisting the help of a leadership coach to help them improve in specific areas or to achieve specific goals. **Striving for significance as a leader follows this path.**

People have been going outside the typical corporate arena and enlisting or recruiting personal or leadership coaches. They want to change, to improve their performance, and to enhance their ability to win! Strive for significance - lead on purpose!

Many world leaders, executives, and innovative managers have also seen the wisdom and a positive return on their investment of time and resources in training and **coaching their employees and future leaders for optimal results**.

Things are changing in the boardrooms, factories, and on the sales floors of businesses across North America and the globe. **Are you?**

Leaders are changing as well, with more women taking on important leadership roles and proving themselves worthy as they inspire other women to follow their lead. Bravo!

People generally experience problems and challenges in their performance for four major reasons:

Poor or inadequate training
Inadequate equipment or support services
Time constraints and poor time management
Motivation

Unfortunately, many of these reasons can be traced back to poor or *uninspired* leadership.

Many 21st Century leaders are moving into applying a coaching role as an effective style and skill in helping their teams grow and succeed. I found it works well!

Leadership coaching in its essence will help you discover the area(s) which are acting as roadblocks for the person being coached.

Leadership coaching can help you turn roadblocks into stepping-stones for increased success, productivity, and a real sense of satisfaction on the job.

Leadership coaching can bring you a sense of satisfaction as the coach, too **– in bringing out the best and in seeing your people productively grow and win!**

One of the most important aspects of your leadership growth and continued success is measured by the investment in your team and the results of those efforts.

"You win, when your people win!"
Bob 'Idea Man' Hooey

I had the opportunity to repeatedly drive this idea home several years back when I was engaged to work with the President and senior management team for one of Canada's 50 Best Managed Companies.

Over a period of four months, we explored ways of helping these men and women hone their leadership skills to better equip and lead their respective teams. **The results were astounding!** The following year they broke the billion-dollar retail sales mark for the first time in their 33-year history.

This is a lesson learned from working with and studying the actions of North America's leaders in various industries, including the volunteer sector. This, coupled with my own experience in a variety of leadership roles, has reinforced my contention that **"You win when your team wins!"**

I trust you will find solid value in what is shared here and create a **significant legacy of leadership**.

Enjoy this publication and apply its wisdom on your personal leadership journey. Let us know how you liked it and where you were able to apply it: bob@ideaman.net

Bob 'Idea Man' Hooey

Table of Contents

Getting started 2
Table of Contents 6
12 idea-rich strategies for 'Bringing out the BEST in your people' 8
A leadership review or check-up 16
Leadership observations 17
Seven laws of leadership 21
Productivity tips 27
What makes them the BEST? 30
Copyright and license notes 32
Disclaimer 34
Bob's B.E.S.T. publications 35
What they say about Bob 'Idea Man' Hooey 37

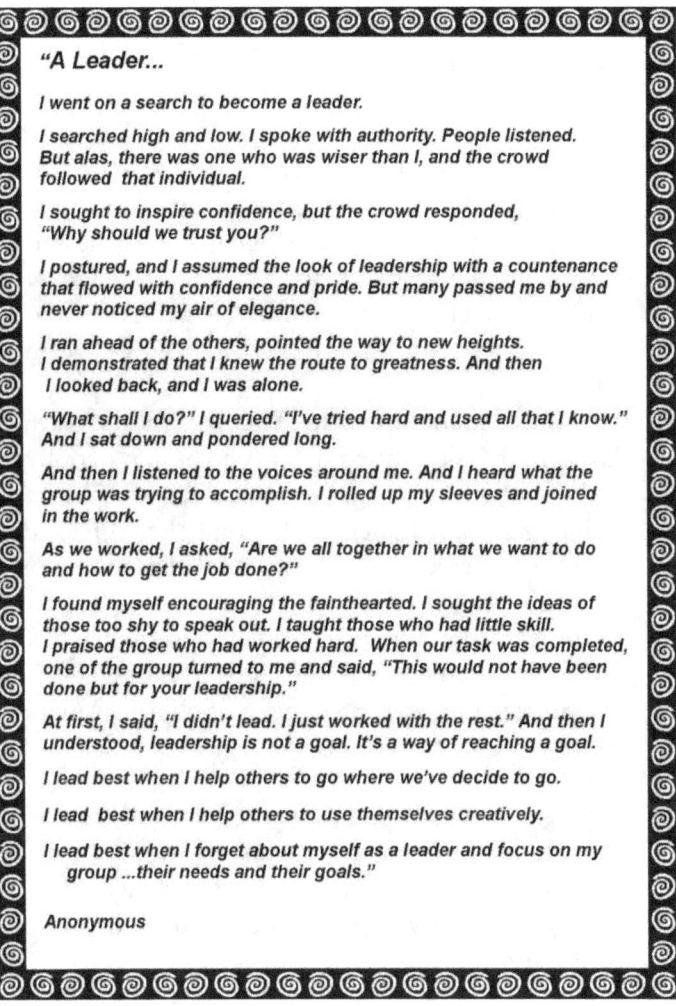

"A Leader...

I went on a search to become a leader.

I searched high and low. I spoke with authority. People listened. But alas, there was one who was wiser than I, and the crowd followed that individual.

I sought to inspire confidence, but the crowd responded, "Why should we trust you?"

I postured, and I assumed the look of leadership with a countenance that flowed with confidence and pride. But many passed me by and never noticed my air of elegance.

I ran ahead of the others, pointed the way to new heights. I demonstrated that I knew the route to greatness. And then I looked back, and I was alone.

"What shall I do?" I queried. "I've tried hard and used all that I know." And I sat down and pondered long.

And then I listened to the voices around me. And I heard what the group was trying to accomplish. I rolled up my sleeves and joined in the work.

As we worked, I asked, "Are we all together in what we want to do and how to get the job done?"

I found myself encouraging the fainthearted. I sought the ideas of those too shy to speak out. I taught those who had little skill. I praised those who had worked hard. When our task was completed, one of the group turned to me and said, "This would not have been done but for your leadership."

At first, I said, "I didn't lead. I just worked with the rest." And then I understood, leadership is not a goal. It's a way of reaching a goal.

I lead best when I help others to go where we've decide to go.

I lead best when I help others to use themselves creatively.

I lead best when I forget about myself as a leader and focus on my group ...their needs and their goals."

Anonymous

I don't know who originally wrote this but include it as it has a solid point if we are serious about honing our abilities to lead, equip and motivate our respective teams.

12 idea-rich strategies for 'Bringing out the BEST in your people'

"Never, never, never, never, never give up!" was the sage advice of **Sir Winston Churchill** in answer to how he successfully led the British people to withstand the might of the Nazi war machine. When faced with a leadership challenge, remember his words and dig in… amazingly enough when you do, so will your team!

Alan Loy McGinnis wrote **'The Time Trap'** early in the last century about bringing out the best in people. It was well-received and gained exposure and acceptance among *progressive* leaders at that time. I've reflected on what he outlined and have his **'12 Rules'** sitting on the wall above my desk as this piece is written. They serve as a *visual guide* and reminder of their importance in leading and coaching the people, *like yourself*, with whom I have the privilege of working with across North America and, more recently, the globe.

If you are *committed* to being an effective leader, perhaps they should be sitting somewhere close, so they are not far from your mind's eye. They are included, *along with my own reflective thoughts*, for your **inspiration, information, and illumination**.

Expect the best from the people you lead

See them performing at their best, even when they are struggling. People will often rise or fall to the level of our expectations and our coaching. See them as they could be, not as they are! **Imagine the possibilities!**

Don't limit them by expecting or accepting less than their best. You owe it to them to set realistic, but challenging expectations. ***They will rise to them!***

You can help them reach these as their leader/coach, cheerleader, or champion. This can be a large challenge when you are a leader faced at working with what seems to be a dysfunctional or fractious team. Your saving grace can be keeping your eye and those you lead on the ultimate or shared goal.

For example, ***General Eisenhower*** *had the challenging role of being the supreme commander in the liberation of Europe during the Second World War. He faced an enemy who was well equipped and motivated to win. He also faced the challenge of working with warring factions within the Allied ranks. He persevered and went on to help us win.*

Make a thorough study of the other person's needs

Each person on your team is an individual with specific skills, talents, strengths, weaknesses, needs, and dreams. Investing the time to get to know them makes it easier to lead and direct them for mutual success. Investing time in understanding and getting to know them also builds strategic bonds which can build bridges to the success and positive performance of them and your team.

Weak leaders lead from the surface. Strong leaders dig deep to learn what best motivates those they lead. They know where to best challenge and direct their skills for success. This allows them to best direct and use the talents and skills of their entire team.

Establish high standards for excellence

Leaders *ultimately* fail when they accept mediocre results or neglect to set challenging standards. As mentioned previously, don't fail your team by allowing them to be *just* ok in their roles.

People will amaze you when you set the bar higher and lead by example. There are valid examples where good enough was appropriate. However, we settle for *seconds* (left-over's) when we could have reached higher, dug deeper, and been more successful. Be realistic but be ready to push past the comfort zone into the winner's zone. The example and standards you set, model, and accept as a leader will determine the growth and success of your team.

Create an environment where failure is not fatal

Mistakes are a *natural part of life* and taking risks means occasionally you fail. If your team feels supported and encouraged, they will begin to take risks and move past their **comfort zone into the winners' zone**.

Help them learn from the lessons of any mistakes and move ahead with energy to face the next challenge.

Help them stretch and grow, knowing that they will make mistakes in their journey, as you did!

"No man (woman) will make a great leader who wants to do it all them self or get all the credit for doing it."
Andrew Carnegie

I remember having one of the clerics in my Tehran, Iran audience take me aside to talk about this. He talked about being a martyr for God. I got more concerned as we talked.

Eventually I said, **"Seems like we are both saying we want our people to take risks."** *He nodded, and I quickly said goodbye and walked away. Whew!*

If they are going anywhere near where you want to go, climb on other people's bandwagons

A *wise* leader is open to letting his team set the pace and direction; provided it takes them along the path towards the eventual goal set by the leader. In this case, you as the leader can become the cheerleader and coach, helping them move along more successfully. *I have frequently found team members had great ideas and their creative input moves us successfully forward.*

Sometimes, however, you need to be honest and realize that people are not going the same direction or share the same values as you. In that case, redirect them or let them go and stay your own course. Be courageous enough to realize that you can follow your own path. Others who share your values will follow.

Employ strategic models to encourage success

This goes to the *heart* of leadership by example. Make sure this is modeled in your own life and in the lives of those you promote and delegate to succeed.

When your team sees it working in your life and actions, they will be more open to allowing change in their own lives and performance.

Recognize and applaud achievement

People do not work *simply* for money. In fact, most of the lists compiled show money much lower on the chart of motivators. Each employee or team member has his or her own needs, desires, and drives. Know them so you can strategically employ and encourage them.

Two of those needs, deep inside each of us are:

The need to feel *appreciated* and important.
The need to feel *included* in the process.

As a leader, the most effective thing we can do is to recognize achievement and effort from those we lead and to share and applaud their achievements. Often small, genuine recognition activities will be more effective than fancy reward programs. The point is to make sure you see what they are doing and let them know you appreciate it. **Hint:** Make sure any recognition is relevant to their needs and desires.

Employ a mixture of positive and negative reinforcement

We understand it is a good thing to provide praise and positive reinforcement in our team members' efforts.

This affirms their actions and encourages them to move ahead. Praise in public.

It is also necessary, at times, to apply the opposite tactic when one of them is doing something detrimental or self-defeating in the fulfillment or follow-through of their role. Letting them know what is **NOT** acceptable is part of a leader's role. We can do it nicely but do it we must; if they are to grow and maximize their potential. Correct in private as your goal here is to help them, not embarrass them.

Appeal *sparingly* to the competitive urge

Each of us has a natural competitive edge. If used wisely, competition for personal growth and success can be a great tool to much higher achievement. However, it has its *dark* side in allowing divisive actions and negative attitudes to creep into a team environment. Focus on the *team accomplishment* and mutual win. Encourage each team member to compete for higher standards and personal skill development.

Place a premium on collaboration

This is where team 'works' and where effective leaders learn to pull people from diverse backgrounds, agendas, and experiences into an effective working unit.

Brainstorming is one way of effective collaboration and team building, allowing each team member to build and draw on the brainpower of another. What you are looking for is adding-value vs. tearing down or unproductive criticism and negativity.

Build into the group an allowance for storms

It is not always smooth sailing as a leader. Surprise, surprise! Storms, difficulties, challenges, detours, and disasters can strike when you least expect them.

*When we were sailing to Japan from Hawaii in summer of 1988, we encountered what the Japanese later told us was a **'baby'** typhoon. I'm sure glad it didn't reach puberty!* ☺

Our captain was an experienced sailor and former US Coast Guard Captain. The other two crew members had deep water experience and had encountered similar storms (but not typhoons).

I had never experienced anything like this as most of my sailing was near coastal or island areas! I was more than a bit nervous, more so when we tipped (lay down) the boat. ☺

Captain John's *commanding leadership, along with the hands-on experience of **Phil** and **Dave** helped us survive this life threatening super-natural phenomenon. We fought the storm for over 13 hours before reaching safer sailing. We dealt with it as needed to survive and to gain our port of Kobe, Japan.*

As a leader, you need to build in allowances for these *speed bumps*, *storms*, and *detours* in your team's progress and have plans in place to cover each potential challenge. Sometimes you need to step in and help them weather the storm.

TEAMWORK
MOTIVATION
INSPIRATION
LEADERSHIP
VISION
+ INNOVATION
─────────────
SUCCESS

Take steps to keep your own motivation high

You are 'on' as a leader all the time. This means people will be looking at you and taking their cue from you. It also means you need to keep your personal motivation high and maintain a positive outward attitude.

This means you may need to find a trusted advisor or coach with whom you can discuss your challenges in private.

Letting your negative feelings show can be devastating to your team. They look to you as being confident, clear in focus, and consistent in action and follow through. Don't disappoint them.

Understand and learn to apply these basic keys (rules) of the leadership road to smooth out your path and make it easier for those who follow you to successfully walk in your footsteps.

"Management is doing things right; leadership is doing the right things."
Peter Drucker

A leadership review or check-up

Reflect on these probing questions around your leadership role, responsibility, and skill. Briefly record your thoughts. Being honest in recognizing your strengths and focused areas of growth is one of the characteristics of the top-level leaders. Asking for help or getting coaching is another idea-rich leadership success characteristic.

What is your *personal vision* for your leadership role?

What are your specific *areas* of responsibility?

What *strengths* and *skills* do you bring to the role?

What leadership areas do you need *help* in developing?

Where do you need to draw on the skills of your fellow leaders or employees? Perhaps engage a leadership or team development coach.

Leadership observations

"Learning is the essential fuel for leaders, the source of high octane energy that keeps up the momentum by continually sparking new understanding, new ideas, and new challenges. It is indispensable under today's conditions of rapid change and complexity. Very simply, those who do not learn do not long survive as leaders."
Warren Bevis & Burt Nanus

Here are some leadership ideas drawn from observations and lessons learned first-hand from a wide range of leaders. I have been blessed with some great role models – leaders in business, industry, association management, community service, Toastmasters, my NSA and CAPS colleagues, and from my parents, my wife, and friends. Here are some **shared characteristics** observed from the leaders in my life and experience.

Leaders are not born

Leaders emerge and need to be nurtured by other leaders who see their potential. Leadership is a learned skill, honed by experience and by finding the inner motivational points that inspire people to assume leadership in various aspects of their lives. Leaders are *revealed* when people see value and follow their direction.

I often saw this first-hand in my Toastmasters and CAPS leadership. When I approached people and asked them to tackle a challenge, they often took personal leadership and championed its eventual success.

Leaders are open to change

Leaders have the courage to **_lead change_** and deal with the turmoil of change. Positive change often happens when someone takes personal leadership and responsibility in a situation and is open to grow.

Leaders develop a sense of adventure and a realization that change is not always a *negative* event. Leaders see themselves as catalysts for innovative change. A true leader will see the plateau or status quo as an opportunity or foundation to move ahead and make positive changes.

Leaders are creative

Leaders are flexible in finding solutions to common challenges. Often it is the creative approach that shows the way out of the problem or mess at hand. This creative outlook may even create new products or entire industries. The leader looks for that creative or innovative *twist* which will unlock the secret to solving the challenge. They are persistent in looking for innovative ways to solve problems and will inspire others to do the same.

Leaders make mistakes and build on lessons learned

Life is about learning and leadership even more so. Leaders take *calculated* risks and sometimes they make mistakes or fail. The difference being, *true* leaders understand this and learn from the experience. This is a great part of the leadership process! Failure fuels their determination to succeed.

They will move ahead, better informed, striving for the next opportunity to **'lead and learn'**.

Leaders are forged in the heat of reality, moulded on the anvil of adversity, by the hammers of life

Personal leadership emerges in the heat of the worst challenges and conditions in your life. You can choose to take personal responsibility for your leadership role and abilities to act. I have seen the most unlikely men and women take this leadership role when the going was tough or the odds overwhelming – and succeed where others simply complained or quit trying. **Leaders don't quit; they quietly find the strength and keep going.**

Leaders are more often readers

This may not hold true of every leader. However, many of those men and women I have grown to respect make *selective* reading a definite part of their leadership growth path. They read outside their own areas of knowledge, experience, and industries. They are open to learn from a myriad of sources. They have found that in a multitude of counsel there is wisdom. *Fortunately for me, they are open to share it.*

Reading allows you to access the wisdom of the ages from leaders long gone as well as from current and emerging thought leaders. Selective, strategic reading provides value-added information that allows you to explore new ideas, new methods, and new ways of thinking. It gives you the leadership and career development ammunition you need to set, stretch, and successfully reach your goals.

Visit: **www.SuccessPublications.ca** for information on Bob's idea-rich leadership, career, and business success publications. Build your own leaders edge success library.

Leaders are the foundation upon which our success is given substance

In my life this is certainly true! I can look back to the pivotal points in my life and often there was the guiding hand of a leader who invested in my life, growth, and well-being.

You might see parallels in your own life and career. So many men and women and organizations have played a role in helping me to hone my talents and enhance my skills which allowed me to discover that I had hidden leadership strengths and skills.

I have been humbled by their investment, their encouragement, and the recognition I have garnered along the way.

"My continued leadership growth and sharing of my leadership lessons are my gift back to them for the faith they showed in my life. Leadership is a 'giving back' life style of choice and commitment."
Bob 'Idea Man' Hooey

Seven laws of leadership

Here is a quick synopsis of my keynote session for 600 plus Alberta mayors, reeves and councillors held in Edmonton, Alberta. These **Seven Laws of Leadership** served as the core part of my remarks at their Annual General Meeting.

Perhaps you've seen the movie **Lincoln**, released in 2012. I did, and it refreshed my appreciation for the amazing role he played during a dark period of challenge. This is where real leadership shines – in the darkness of a tremendous seemingly unsolvable challenge.

President Abraham Lincoln *led the Northern States through one of the bloodiest and darkest pages in US history. He saw the concept of keeping both sides together as something worth fighting for… and fight he did! Sadly, he did not live to see his dream of a re-unified United States take place. His focused leadership laid the foundations for this outcome.*

His *legacy of leadership* lives on in the proud nation and neighbours to our south.

I visited Ford Theater, where he was shot, a few years back while speaking in the area. I sat *quietly* in the seats below *his* box to get a true sense of the place. I imagined how the evening played out. I toured the basement museum where they had gathered many items, including his blood-spattered clothing. I have a much greater respect for the challenges he faced.

As leaders we will face challenges, both external and internal. Our character and our skills will be revealed and polished as we face each one. Those we would lead will look 'to' us and 'at' us in this respect.

Here are some areas of consideration (Leadership laws) I feel necessary for us to be effective and influential leaders. They are:

Example – people need to be able to depend on your leadership.

Today, more than ever, people are looking for leaders who will lead by example in their dealings with people and their lifestyles.

Communication – people need to know what you are saying.

Today, more than ever, people are looking for clarity and consistency in our written and oral communications. They are looking for honesty and openness in the dialogue they have with us as leaders.

Ability – you need to be capable of leading other people.

Today, more than ever, people are looking for more than a slick appearance. They want content and proven ability they can trust to get them through the increasing challenges of the 21st Century.

Motivation – you need to know why YOU want to be a leader.

Today, more than ever, people want to know *'why'* you are doing what you are doing and so do you! A simple *trust me* won't cut it. This is even more noticeable with the current crop of 16 – 24-year old's who are affectionately dubbed, "Generation WHY?"

Authority – people need to respond to your leadership.

Today, more than ever, people want to be able to see demonstrated commitment and power in your decisions and authority in your actions.

Strategy – you need to know where you are going.

Today, more than ever, people want to know you have a plan; one that is well thought out, covering all the contingencies and challenges. They frequently want to know the details of that strategy before they agree to follow you.

Love and compassion – you need to care for the people around you.

Today, more than ever, people want to know and see that you truly care about them, their needs, their concerns, their fears, their dreams, and their well-being. Lip service, hype, or idle words will not cut it on the 21st Century leadership track.

Take a serious look at your current leadership skill levels considering these seven laws.

Creative Leaders Win!

Here are some objectives and benefits of *unleashing* your creative and constructive leadership:

More accurate information – increased productivity facilitated by better communication.

Effective coordination of activities – *"How do I fit in the big picture?"* – decreased duplication and wasted resources.

Improving the flow of ideas - both internally (up and down) and externally – generating better buy-in and team energies.

Facilitating the decision-making process – being an agent of change not just being on the receiving end of change.

Training – cross training, uniform training, and an interactive forum for an honest exchange of ideas and feedback.

Building morale – encouraging teamwork and mutual support which has a direct impact on morale within an organization.

Accomplishment of these objectives will assist you in being a more effective leader and in creatively helping you to prepare your team to win.

Occasionally, we need to pause, to refocus, to gain a higher perspective, to make sure we are still leading in the right direction. If we are not going where we want in pursuit of our focus and goals, our efficiency and effectiveness will be misdirected and disappointing.

Pause, refocus, and redirect!

Two creative leadership lessons

One of the biggest lessons about leadership and creative problem solving: **there is ALWAYS a solution!** In fact, frequently, there are **a multitude of solutions.**

Leadership development, with its respective challenges, is no different. There are a multitude of opportunities to support and reinforce your abilities and skills in leading and helping your team navigate the challenges you share. This is where you bring your creativity to bear.

If your leadership problem is *industry specific* you might want to talk to others in your industry and **"Thunder-think"** (*Bob's version of brainstorming*) some answers or bring it to your next Chamber of Commerce, trade, or professional association meeting.

The second lesson: **You are not the ONLY one with a problem**.

While I served on the National Speakers Association's **Chapter Leadership Council** *we often shared challenges our respective Chapters were encountering. Someone usually had a suggestion that would help which we could pass along.*

Sharing a problem can lead to finding the *key* to solving it. Someone not directly involved in your problem may see a solution or thread that unravels it, due to the difference in his or her perspective or experience.

Because they are not *emotionally* involved, they can see it with objectivity and perhaps more clarity! **Be open to ask for help!**

I believe passionately in the information I present and enjoy the opportunity to pass on my lessons; learned, at times, from magnificent failures.

I'd love to share and see my **Ideas At Work!** directly or indirectly with you and your team members. I trust you will find it valuable. Our primary priority and purpose is to see you succeed and do whatever possible to facilitate that leadership process.

At **Ideas At Work**! — we want to see you use this information in your dealings with each other and in serving the needs your teams and clients. **Call us to explore how we can help you and your teams.**

Connect with Bob 'Idea Man' Hooey:

Facebook: www.facebook.com/bob.hooey
Success Publications: www.SuccessPublications.ca
Websites: www.ideaman.net www.BobHooey.training
LinkedIn:
www.linkedin.com/in/canadianideamanbobhooey
YouTube: www.youtube.com/ideamanbob
Smashwords:
www.smashwords.com/profile/view/Hooey
Email: bob@ideaman.net
Creative Office: 780-736-0009
Snail mail: PO Box 10, Egremont, AB T0A0Z0

Productivity tips

A few years back, I had the pleasure of spending a couple of hours with Darren Hardy, *Publisher of **"Success magazine, What Achievers Read"***. Our discussion topic was how we could be more productive as leaders and entrepreneurs. This topic is very near to my heart and I took *copious* notes as he shared his ideas and stories with us. I decided to pass along a few highlights from memory.

He challenged us to **'*say NO*'** more often and to narrow our focus and investment of time to the vital few functions that ***only we*** could do. He challenged us to cut back on where we **'*say YES*'** if we were serious about our productivity. He challenged us to move from **Reactive to Creative** and to delegate everything we could to free up time for pursuit of what is more vital in our lives. Bravo!

He's met and interviewed some of the world's top performers for his magazine. He went on to share examples of super-achievers who put some of these ideas into practice. **Sir Richard Branson** would work on only 3 strategic priorities at a time. Apple founder **Steve Jobs** learned the power of working only one BIG thing at a time and would focus for 3 hours on his number one priority. **Warren Buffet**, on average, only took 1 of 100 deals offered to him.

Darren suggested we should move from **Labour to Leadership**. He actually said everything ***we DO*** is keeping us from what we should be doing.

This rang true for me as I had just presented in Ottawa at a national food and beverage conference for a group of club managers. I had challenged them to focus on what was the most critical part of their role and built on their expertise and experience. I had challenged them to invest time training their staff, so they could delegate the less critical activities to them.

He quoted **Kenneth Cole**, "*Success has less to do with what we can get ourselves to do and more to do with **keeping ourselves from doing what we shouldn't.***" I looked down at my *stylish* Kenneth Cole watch and smiled. This too hit home, as I tend to be excited about ideas and making them work. I say yes too easily, often, to ideas which don't move my career or business forward. Point well taken, Darren!

He quoted from an interview with Steve Jobs where Steve said, *"I am as proud of what we **don't do** as what we do."* He quoted from one of my favourite management gurus, **Peter Drucker** who said, *"There is nothing so useless as doing efficiently, that which shouldn't be done at all."* **Ouch!**

He challenged me again, as a leader and entrepreneur, to determine my vital few functions (that only I can do), my high impact priorities, and measurements to monitor and track my progress. *"This clarity would help in my quest to be more effective in what I do and, in my pursuit, to help my readers and audiences grow and succeed."*

My plan is to do exactly that. I will be setting aside time to revisit my websites with an eye to adding more *clarity* in what I offer, and in what activities I engage to assist my clients, colleagues and community.

I pass along his challenge to you, my new friend and reader; in the hopes that what is shared in **'LEAD!' and in our deeper 'Legacy of Leadership'** book will be a benefit for your growth and success as well as your life of significance. Visit www.SuccessPublications.ca to order.

Darren shared these points. **Don't mistake:**

Movement for **Achievement**
Activity for **Productivity**
Rushing for **Results**

I've heard variations of these, perhaps you have too. I felt they were worth repeating. Wishing you all the success and satisfaction in becoming a more effective and influential leader in your field.

"Passion is energy. Feel the power that comes from focusing on what excites you." **Oprah Winfrey**

Bring Bob 'Idea Man' Hooey in to work with you and your leadership team.

Perhaps your organization would like to bring Bob in to train, coach, and share a few leadership success ideas with your team. **Call him today: 1-888-848-8407** Toll-Free North America or Email him at: bob@ideaman.net

Visit: **www.ideaman.net or www.BobHooey.training** for more information on his innovative leadership development programs. He can help you make a positive difference with your leadership and in your team's growth and performance.

What makes them the BEST?

"Leadership at its 'best' is about developing other strong leaders." **Bob 'Idea Man' Hooey**

Each year companies from across Canada apply to be judged for this challenging designation. Each year a few make it, and some re-qualify, to be named as **Canada's 50 Best Managed Companies**.

Sustained success in any field is built on a solid foundation of strategic, inspirational leadership. Focused leadership sets the pace, fuels the growth, and equips and motivates the team to succeed. Leaders cannot accomplish this alone, but they are the key in its accomplishment. **What have you done to lead, assist, and motivate your team to succeed today?**

I've had the privilege of working with senior executives from this well-deserved group of companies. I've seen first-hand their leadership in action and the positive, profitable, and productive results it inspired.

Here are four crucial areas with twelve focused points created in a keeper card when one of the companies I worked with achieved this goal. We had a challenge drawing down to these 12 pivotal points, so we could create a business sized laminate card for each of their nearly 7,000 employees across Canada as well as those who attended the ceremony.

They shared these points that evening in their continued **Striving for Excellence** focus.

Building

Bridges not barriers or boundaries
Profitable client and supplier relationships
Success via long term vision and value

Empowered employees

Putting their enthusiasm and energy to work
Committed to excellence in serving our clients
Providing inspired 'by example' leadership

Strategic

Thinking in focus, value, and action
Recruiting and promoting the 'right' leaders
Alliances with strong leaders and companies

Training

Employees to succeed in and on the job
Initiative and innovation in client service
Executives in honing their leadership skills

Perhaps you can leverage from these points or create your own. Having some simple points of focus will help you keep on track in your efforts to better serve your team, enhance your leadership, and build a successful team and organization.

Embrace and enjoy your leadership journey. It will challenge you, but the results will be worth your investment of time and energy.

Copyright and license notes

LEAD!
12 idea-rich leadership success secrets

Bob 'Idea Man' Hooey, *Accredited Speaker, 2011 Spirit of CAPS recipient. Prolific author of 30 plus business, leadership, and career success publications*

© Copyright 1999-2018 Bob 'Idea Man' Hooey

All rights reserved worldwide *No part of this publication may be retained, copied, sold, rented or loaned, transmitted, reproduced, broadcast, performed or distributed in any such medium, or by any means, nor stored in any computer or distributed over any network without permission in writing from the publisher and/or author. Care has been taken to trace ownership of copyright material contained in this volume. Graphics are royalty free or under license. The publisher will gladly receive information that will allow him to rectify any reference or credit line in subsequent editions. Segments of this publication were originally published as articles and/or parts of other books and program materials and are included here by permission of the publishers and authors.* Unattributed quotations are by Bob 'Idea Man' Hooey.

Cover design: **Wendy** (craftarc)
Photos of Bob: **Dov Friedman**,
www.photographybyDov.com
Bonnie-Jean McAllister, www.elantraphotography.com
Editorial, layout and design: **Irene Gaudet**, Vitrak Creative Services, vitrakcreative.com

ISBN 13: 978-1986737708   ISBN 10: 1986737705

Printed in the United States 10 9 8 7 6 5 4 3 2 1
Success Publications – a division of Creativity Corner Inc.
Box 10, Egremont, Alberta, Canada T0A 0Z0
www.successpublications.ca
Creative office: 1-780-736-0009

Acknowledgements, credits, and disclaimers

As with each of my books, a very special dedication of this piece of myself, to the two people who meant the most to me, my folks **Ron and Marge Hooey**. Sadly, both my parents left this earthly realm in 1999. I still miss our time together and your encouragement and love. I was blessed with the two of you in my life. I've added **George and Lillian Sidor** (Irene's folks).

To my inspiring wife and professional proof reader and publications coach, **Irene Gaudet**, who loves, encourages, and supports me in my quest to continue sharing my **Ideas At Work!** across the world. Thank you seems so inadequate for your timely work in helping make my writing and my client service better! I love the time we spend together!

To my colleagues and friends in the National Speakers Association (NSA), the Canadian Association of Professional Speakers (CAPS), and the Global Speakers Federation (GSF) who continually challenge me to strive for success and increased excellence.

To my great audiences, leaders, students, coaching clients, and readers across the globe who share their experiences and enjoyment of my work. Your positive and supportive feedback encourages me to keep working on additional programs and success publications like this updated version. My experience with you creates the foundation for additional real-life experiences I can take from the stage to the page, the classroom to the boardroom.

My thanks to a select few friends for your ongoing support and 'constructive' abuse. You know who you are. ☺

Disclaimer

We have not attempted to cite all the authorities and sources consulted in the preparation of this book. To do so would require much more space than is available. The list would include departments of various governments, libraries, industrial institutions, periodicals, and many individuals. Inspiration was drawn from many sources, including other books by the author; in this updated creation of 'LEAD!'

This book is written and designed to provide information on more effective use of your time, as a life and leadership enhancement guide. It is sold with the 'explicit' understanding that the publisher and/or the author are not engaged in rendering legal, accounting, or other Professional services. If legal or other expert assistance is required, the services of a competent Professional in your geographic area should be sought.

It is not the purpose of this book to reprint all the information that is otherwise available. Its primary purpose is to complement, amplify, and supplement other books and reference materials already available. You are encouraged to search out and study all the available material, learn as much as possible, and tailor the information to your individual needs. This will help to enhance your success in being a more effective sales person, leader or professional.

Every effort has been made to make this book as complete and as accurate as possible within the scope of its focus. However, there may be mistakes, both typographical and in content or attribution. Graphics are royalty free or under license. Care has been taken to trace ownership of copyright material contained in this volume. The publisher will gladly receive information that will allow him to rectify any reference or credit line in subsequent editions. This book should be used only as a general guide and not as the ultimate source of information. Furthermore, this book contains information that is current only up to the date of publication.

The purpose of 'LEAD!' is to educate and entertain; perhaps to inform and to inspire. *It is certainly to challenge its readers to learn and apply its secrets and tips, to challenge them to enhance their skills and leverage their time to create more Productive outcomes. The author and publisher shall have neither liability nor responsibility to any person or entity with respect to any loss or damage caused, or alleged to have been caused, directly or indirectly, by the information contained in this book.*

Bob's B.E.S.T. publications

Bob is a prolific author who has been capturing and sharing his wisdom and experience in print and electronic formats for the past fifteen plus years. In addition to the following publications, several of them best sellers, he has written for consumer, corporate, professional associations, trade, and on-line publications. He has been engaged to write and assist on publications by other best-selling writers and successful companies.

Bob's **B**usiness **E**nhancement **S**uccess **T**ools

Leadership, business, and career success series
Running TOO Fast (8th edition 2018)
Legacy of Leadership (3rd edition 2016)
Make ME Feel Special! (6th edition 2016)
Why Didn't I 'THINK' of That? (5th edition 2015)
Speaking for Success! (8th edition 2016)
THINK Beyond the First Sale (3rd edition 2017)
Prepare Yourself to WIN! (3rd edition 2018)

Bob's mini-book success series
The Courage to Lead! (4th edition 2017)
Creative Conflict (3rd edition 2017)
Get to YES! (3rd edition 2017)
THINK Before You Ink! (3rd edition 2017)
Running to Win! (2nd edition 2017)
How to Generate More Sales (4th edition 2017)
Unleash your Business Potential (3rd edition 2017)

Learn to Listen (2nd edition 2017)
Creativity Counts! (3rd edition 2016)
Create Your Future! (3rd edition 2017)

Bob's Pocket Wisdom series

Pocket Wisdom for Selling Professionals
Pocket Wisdom for Speakers
Pocket Wisdom for Innovators
Pocket Wisdom for Leaders – Power of One!
Pocket Wisdom for Business Builders

Co-authored books created by Bob

Quantum Success – 3 volume series (2006)
In the Company of Leaders (3rd edition 2014)
Foundational Success (2nd edition 2013)

Bob's Idea-rich leaders edge series (2018)

LEAD! *12 idea-rich leadership success strategies*
CREATE! *Idea-rich strategies for enhanced innovation*
TIME! *Idea-rich tips for enhanced performance and productivity*
SERVICE! *Idea-rich strategies for enhanced customer service*
SPEAK! *Idea-rich tips and techniques for great presentations*
CREATIVE CONFLICT! *Idea-rich leadership strategies for team success*

Visit: www.SuccessPublications.ca for more information on Bob's publications and other leadership and business success resources.

**Email: bob@ideaman.net
or visit: www.SuccessPublications.ca**

What they say about Bob 'Idea Man' Hooey

As I travel across North America, and more recently around the globe, sharing my Ideas At Work!, I am fortunate to get feedback and comments from my audiences and colleagues. These comments come from people who have been touched, challenged, or simply enjoyed themselves in one of my sessions.

I'd love to come and share some ideas with your organization and teams.

"I still get comments from people about your presentation. Only a few speakers have left an impression that lasts that long. You hit a spot with the tourism people." **Janet Bell**, Yukon Economic Forums

"Thank you, Bob, it is always a pleasure to see a true professional at work. You have made the name 'Speaker' stand out as a truism - someone who encourages people to examine their lives and adjust. The personal stories you shared with your audience made such a great impression on everyone. The comments indicated you hit people right where it is important - in their hearts. Each of those in your audience took away a new feeling of personal success and encouragement." **Sherry Knight**, Dimension Eleven Human Resources

"I am pleased to recommend Bob 'Idea Man' Hooey to any organization looking for a charismatic, confident speaker and seminar leader. I have seen Bob in action on several occasions, and he is ALWAYS on! Bob has the ability to grab his audience's attention and keep it. Quite simply, if Bob is involved - your program or seminar is guaranteed to succeed." **Maurice Laving**, Coordinator Training and Development, London Drugs

"Last week Bob set the tone for our two-day leadership meeting and gave us all a motivational lift. *His compassion and true interest in people was clearly evident, making him very credible. He shared some great stories, has a wealth of experience and knowledge and it was a pleasure listening to him. His down-to-Earth style makes it easier to retain the information presented. He also followed up with additional info and handouts, cementing his message of building bridges, not walls. Fantastic job, Bob, and thanks again!"* **Barbara Afra Beler**, MBA, Senior Specialist Commercial Community, Alberta North, **BMO Bank of Montreal**

*"I have been so excited working with Bob Hooey, as he has given inspiration and motivation to our leadership team members. Both at the Brick Warehouse – Alberta and here at Art Van Furniture – Michigan; with his years of experience in working with business executives and his humorous and delightful packaging of his material, he makes **learning with Bob a real joy**. But most importantly, anyone who encounters his material is the better for it."* **Kim Yost**, CEO Art Van Furniture, former CEO The Brick

Motivate your teams, your employees, and your leaders to 'productively' grow and 'profitably' succeed!

Protect your conference investment - leverage your training dollars.

Enhance your professional career and sell more products and services.

Equip and motivate your leaders and their teams to grow and succeed, 'even' in tough times!

Leverage your time to enhance your skills, equip your teams, and better serve your clients.

Leverage your leadership and investment of time to leave a significant legacy!

Call today to engage best-selling author, award winning, inspirational leadership keynote speaker, leaders' success coach, and employee development trainer, **Bob 'Idea Man' Hooey** and his innovative, audience based, results-focused, **Ideas At Work!** for your next company, convention, leadership, staff, training, or association event. You'll be glad you did!

Call 1-780-736-0009 to connect with Bob 'Idea Man' Hooey today!

Learn more about Bob at: **www.ideaman.net** or **www.BobHooey.training**

www.ingramcontent.com/pod-product-compliance
Lightning Source LLC
Chambersburg PA
CBHW030101230526
45471CB00003B/1201